THE
DRUGS TRADE
THE IMPACT ON OUR LIVES

LOUIE FOOKS

HODDER
Wayland

an imprint of Hodder Children's Books

21st Century Debates Series

Genetics • Surveillance • Internet • Media • Artificial Intelligence • Climate Change • Energy • Rainforests • Waste, Recycling and Reuse • Endangered Species • Air Pollution • An Overcrowded World? • Food Supply • Water Supply • World Health • Global Debt • Terrorism • New Religious Movements • Racism • Violence in Society • Globalisation • Tourism • Transportation

Produced for Hodder Wayland by White-Thomson Publishing Ltd,
2/3 St Andrew's Place, Lewes, East Sussex BN7 1UP

Published in Great Britain in 2003 by Hodder Wayland, an imprint of Hodder Children's Books.

Project editor: Kelly Davis
Commissioning editor: Steve White-Thomson
Proofreader: David C. Sills, Proof Positive Reading Service
Series and book design: Chris Halls, Mind's Eye Design
Picture research: Shelley Noronha, Glass Onion Pictures

British Library Cataloguing in Publication Data
Fooks, Louie
   The Drugs Trade. - (21st Century Debates)
   1. Drug traffic - Juvenile literature
   I. Title
   363.4'5
ISBN 0 7502 4065 2

Printed in Hong Kong

Hodder Children's Books, a division of Hodder Headline Ltd, 338 Euston Road, London NW1 3BH

Picture credits: Impact 4, 21 and 49 (Vera Lentz), 36 (Simon Shepheard), 39 (Piers Cavendish), 40 (Rupert Gonant), 50 (Christopher Pillitz), 58 (Andy Johnstone); James Davis Travel Photography – cover background; Photofusion 37 (Paul Doyl), 42 (Christa Stadtler), 53 (David Tothill), 59 (Ute Klaphake); Popperfoto 7 (Mike Hutchings), 9, 23, 25 (Karl Penhaul), 28, 30, 31 (Pascal Rossignol), 32, 33, 34 (Jason Reed), 35 (Colin Braley), 44, 46 (Javier Casella), 55 (Muzzamil Pasha), cover foreground (Pascal Rossignol); Rex Features 11 (Greg Smith), 57 (Stuart Clarke); Science Photo Library 5 (Jim Varney), 15 (Cordelia Molloy), 17 and 19 (Tek Image), 18 (Garry Watson), 41; Topham 10, 12, 26, 38, 47, 54; WTPix 6.

Cover: foreground picture shows French customs officers displaying ecstasy tablets, seized at Calais in 1998; background picture shows a marijuana plant.

CONTENTS

The Global Drugs Trade 4

Illegal Drugs 14

Production of Illegal Drugs 20

Traffic! 28

Who Uses Illegal Drugs? 36

Looking Towards Solutions 44

What Else Can Be Done? 52

Glossary 60

Books to Read 62

Useful Addresses 63

Index 64

THE GLOBAL DRUGS TRADE

Most people are very aware of the sale and use of illegal drugs these days. You may have been offered drugs at the school gates or when you are out with your friends. Through newspapers and TV you probably know something about the problems of addiction, and you may have heard reports of seizures of illegal drugs by police and customs officials. The scale of illegal drug use is such that it is often described as an 'epidemic', and governments in some countries have been talking about the need for a 'war on drugs'.

There is certainly a feeling that drug use is out of control and that 'something must be done about it'. What may be more difficult to understand, however, are the factors which fuel this sophisticated illegal trade. It is a trade which links the Afghan poppy farmer or Bolivian coca grower,

A Peruvian farmer puts coca leaves out to dry before they are processed into powder.

through a complex system of production and distribution, to a heroin addict on the streets of London or a lawyer in New York using cocaine. And individuals, organizations and governments often have very different ideas about how best to deal with the many issues it raises.

This book will look in-depth at the production, trafficking and use of illegal drugs and explore some of the strategies which are being used, or suggested, to tackle the problem.

The scale of the global drugs trade

The trade in illegal drugs affects the lives of many millions of people around the world. About 180 million people are estimated to be using illegal drugs, with 144 million taking cannabis, and 50 million using 'harder' drugs such as heroin, cocaine and amphetamines (many people will use both hard and soft drugs). Many more people, in both the developed and the developing world, are involved with the drugs trade, through their part in the production, trafficking and sale of illegal drugs – even if they do not use drugs directly themselves. It is very difficult to measure the size of the global drugs trade and figures produced by different organizations vary enormously. The United Nations Drug Control Programme (UNDCP), however, estimates that the drugs trade is worth up to US$500 billion a year – more than the global tourist industry.

> **FACT**
>
> During the 1990s, consumption of the main problem drugs in developed countries has been stable or declining. The abuse of cocaine fell in North America as compared to a decade earlier and heroin abuse was stable in Western Europe.

A businessman in a developed country snorts lines of cocaine at his office desk. His stressful job probably increases his desire for the 'buzz' of taking cocaine, and his high income means that he can afford to buy regular supplies of the drug.

FACT

In Denmark many young people drink beer, wine and spirits. A survey published in 1995 showed that 96 per cent of Danish fifteen- to sixteen-year-olds were consumers of alcohol.

In the developed world, despite the highly publicized health risks, young women are taking up smoking at a faster rate than young men.

What do we mean by drugs?

So what do we mean by a (non-medicinal) 'drug'? And how is an illegal drug defined? It seems obvious that cocaine and heroin are drugs – and that they are illegal. But could tobacco, alcohol and caffeine also be described as addictive drugs? How harmful are they? And should they themselves be illegal?

Illegal drugs are generally defined by international agreements, drawn up by the United Nations, and endorsed by its member countries. This means that there is general acceptance between countries that drugs such as heroin, cocaine or amphetamines are illegal and must not be produced, sold or used. The main international agreements which control drugs are: the 1961 Single Convention on Narcotic Drugs, the 1971 Convention on Psychotropic Substances, and the 1988 Convention Against Illicit Traffic in Narcotic Drugs and Psychotropic Substances.

In contrast, however, many legal 'drugs' and stimulants, such as alcohol and cigarettes, are widely accepted in the UK, USA and other industrialized countries, and are an important part of many people's everyday lives. But these legal substances can be extremely harmful to the people who take them. Through related health problems, such as heart disease and liver failure, alcohol causes significantly more deaths every year than drug use – 40,000 in the UK (as opposed to less than 1,300 for drugs); and a quarter of American men and 5 per cent of American women will have problems related to alcohol at some stage in their lives. Tobacco is the main cause of at least a third of all cancers (most notably lung cancer), and smoking is directly responsible for about 300,000 deaths each year in the USA and 150,000 in the UK. Many people are also addicted to prescription drugs, such as Valium or Prozac, which may be given to them legally by their doctor.

A Rastafarian lights up a marijuana pipe.

In other societies, drugs that are illegal under international law are actually an important part of social and cultural life and are widely used and accepted. For instance, coca leaves (from which cocaine and crack are derived) are chewed by people in Peru, Colombia and Bolivia, to combat hunger and tiredness. And the smoking of cannabis is widespread in South Africa and the Caribbean.

FACT

A report published in 2002 estimated that thirteen million Britons had taken illegal drugs, and four million Britons had dealt illegal drugs.

Drugs like coca and cannabis are an essential part of everyday life for the communities who use them and they are not thought of as being particularly harmful. In most countries alcohol is widely used and accepted in pubs, restaurants and private homes but it is illegal in Muslim countries such as Saudi Arabia – and, according to the Qur'an, Muslims are not supposed to drink alcohol at all.

What is considered to be illegal or unacceptable has also changed over time. While you may think of drug use as a 'modern' issue, in fact people have used drugs for centuries for medicinal or religious reasons, or to help them relax and enjoy themselves – and these drugs were not necessarily illegal or unacceptable. The original recipe for Coca-Cola contained small amounts of cocaine which was seen as a stimulant rather than a drug. In the nineteenth century many British and North American people, including several famous writers and intellectuals, were addicted to opium, which was cheap and freely available at the time. In fact levels of use in the nineteenth century are thought to have been higher than they are now. At the end of the nineteenth century, however, stronger and more highly addictive substances began to be refined and manufactured, which led to greater concern about drug use and to the introduction of the first international controls on drugs.

Myths and stereotypes

The issue of illegal drugs is surrounded by a number of myths and stereotypes. The stereotyped image of a drug taker may be of a street person in a large industrial city addicted to heroin, stealing to get their next 'fix'. In fact, people who take drugs come from all walks of life, including professionals, women and older people, and there is no such thing as a 'typical' drug user.

Drug users can range from the urban professional taking cocaine in a nightclub or the teenage ecstasy user from a comfortable suburban home, to street children sniffing glue to make their lives more bearable in the shanty towns of Latin America or the Caribbean. There are also many people living along the drug trafficking routes in Asia who are themselves addicted to opium.

Opium-smokers in around 1900 at a high-class opium house in Canton, China.

It is also a widely held belief that people who experiment with 'soft' drugs, such as cannabis, are likely to go on to take 'harder' drugs such as heroin or cocaine. Cannabis is the most widely used drug in the world (over 140 million users) and most of these people will not go on to take hard drugs. In fact, although the typical image of a 'drug user' may be someone using a hypodermic needle, only 3 per cent of drug users ever inject a drug into their bloodstream.

A homeless man living under the Williamsburg Bridge, Brooklyn, New York, 1999. Many homeless people take drugs in order to cope with their harsh living conditions and sense of isolation.

The impact of the global drugs trade

Should we then question the whole idea that drug use is 'out of control'? If individuals choose to take drugs (cannabis, for instance, is widely accepted in several countries, and legal drugs such as tobacco are actually extremely harmful), is there really cause for the current level of concern over illegal drug use?

Certainly some of the language used to talk about the 'drugs epidemic' or the 'war on drugs' seems to suggest that it is a problem that is spiralling out of control. Yet, in developed countries at least, drug use may be relatively stable. Cocaine abuse has been falling in the USA and levels of heroin abuse in Western Europe are now stable.

However, the trade in illegal drugs does have a profound impact on all aspects of our lives. The need for individuals to raise cash to support their drug habits is one reason for the high number of muggings, car crimes and burglaries in our societies. The United Nations (UN) believes that in some countries heavy drug users commit more than 50 per cent of all thefts. The USA's Drug Enforcement Agency reports that 75 per cent of adult males arrested in New York City in 1999 for committing a violent crime tested positive for drug use. And it is estimated that it costs £15,000 a year for a British user to support a heroin habit – a factor contributing to the high level of crime in Britain.

VIEWPOINT

'I used to think I took drugs because I liked them... then I understood it was because I couldn't cope with my feelings.'
Caroline. UK

Police in Houston, USA, make an arrest during an anti-crack operation in 1991.

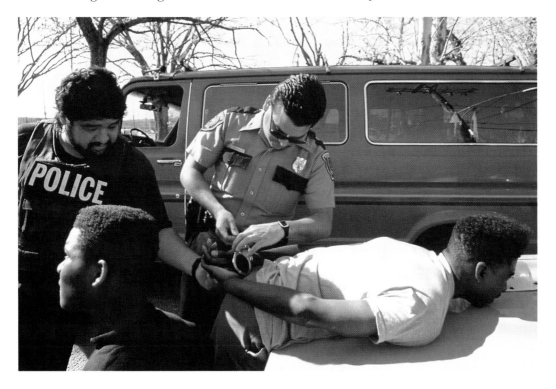

Apart from crime, drug abuse has serious effects on individuals and families. Regular users of heroin, for example, will probably not be able to keep a job, maintain social relations with friends, will expose themselves to serious health risks such as HIV and hepatitis C, and will find it very difficult to take care of a family. Although it is possible for hard drug users to look after children adequately, the US Drug Enforcement Agency claims that 80 per cent of American families reported for maltreatment of children experienced problems with drug abuse. Repeated use of 'hard' drugs such as cocaine and heroin can cause physical and mental harm to users and may well lead to overdose and death.

Education is one way of reducing the demand for illegal drugs in developed countries. Here, an American policeman speaks to fourth graders about the dangers of drugs.

Enormous sums of money are spent every year on the enforcement of international drugs laws. In the USA the federal drug control budget is now more than $15 billion, a fourfold increase over ten years.

Many people think this is too high a price to pay, and question what this money achieves. Perhaps it would be better spent on health and social welfare programmes? Certainly, over the past twenty-five years in the United States, while enforcement of drug prohibition has expanded dramatically, trends in drug production and consumption have remained the same and the prices of cocaine and heroin have more than halved.

Throughout this book we will be looking at the effectiveness of the different strategies used to reduce the production and sale of drugs. In particular we will look at policies which attempt to stop the flow of drugs at source, by hampering production, as well as policies which try to manage and limit the demand for drugs. Finally, we will also weigh up the argument that legalization of drugs might be a more effective way to tackle availability and use than prohibition. The problems associated with illegal drugs are complex and hard to solve, however, and at the moment there do not seem to be any easy answers.

Average annual percentage of population over the age of fifteen abusing heroin and other opiates

Country	Percentage
Iran	2.8
Pakistan	1.7
Australia	0.7
UK	0.6
North America	0.5
Vietnam	0.4
Denmark	0.3
Netherlands	0.2

Source: *Global Illicit Drug Trends 2001*, United Nations Office for Drug Control and Crime Prevention

weblinks

For more information about international drug control issues go to www.waylinks.co.uk/series/21debates/drugstrade

DEBATE

What is your own experience of illegal drugs? Have you ever been offered illegal drugs, or taken them? What influenced your decision to try illegal drugs, or not? Did you learn anything from the experience, and what would you say about illegal drugs to other young people?

ILLEGAL DRUGS

VIEWPOINT

'To many people they [drugs] are alarming and dangerous, and their effects on the lives of people they know, or at least know about, are usually damaging and sometimes catastrophic. To others, particularly those under the age of 30, the drugs ... seem no more dangerous than alcohol... The first group's views are largely based on what they have read and heard. The younger generation's views are largely based on personal experience, or at least on the experience of their friends. Neither group can understand why the other can be so misguided.'

Drugs: Dilemmas and Choices, *Royal College of Psychiatrists, 2000*

This chapter looks at some of the drugs that are most widely known and used in developed countries. This list is by no means comprehensive. Please see the Useful Addresses (page 63) and the weblinks in this chapter for further information.

Amphetamines

Amphetamines are synthetic (manufactured) stimulants, also known as 'uppers'. They usually come as a white, grey or pink powder, or as a putty-like substance known as 'base'. The powder form can be snorted, mixed in a drink, or prepared for injection. Base can be injected or swallowed. During the 1990s, amphetamines were popular on the dance scene and they are probably the next most commonly used illegal drug after cannabis. Amphetamines increase breathing rate, stimulate the heartbeat and may also raise blood pressure. Users may feel more confident, sociable and energetic. However the side-effects include anxiety, irritability and depression. Longer-term usage can cause psychological addiction (a sense of mental and emotional dependency), and regular use often leads to sleeplessness, lack of appetite, and reduced resistance to disease. The strong 'upper' effect can be particularly dangerous for people who have heart or blood pressure problems.

ATS

Amphetamine-type stimulants (ATS) are mainly amphetamine/metamphetamine and ecstasy and are chemically related. In Thailand, the Philippines, Japan, the Republic of Korea and, to a lesser extent, Taiwan, ATS play a similar role to that of opiates in Europe or cocaine in the Americas. ATS abuse is now estimated to affect some 33 million people worldwide.

Cannabis

Cannabis comes from the plant cannabis sativa. Cannabis herb, also known as marijuana, grass, and by many other names, is the dried leaves of the plant and is usually smoked on its own or with tobacco. Hashish is the dark sticky resin made from the plant and is eaten or smoked. Cannabis is a hallucinogen (which means that it distorts the way the mind perceives things) but it can also be classed as a relaxant. It has a mildly sedative effect, which leads to decreased blood pressure, increased appetite, feelings of relaxation, mild intoxication (as in drunkenness), and increased sociability. Using cannabis can make people feel anxious, nervous, depressed and confused. There is no evidence that long-term use leads to physical addiction (in which the body needs or craves it), although some users may be psychologically addicted. Long-term use of cannabis can cause respiratory disorders associated with smoking.

weblinks

For a glossary and more information about legal and illegal drugs go to www.waylinks.co.uk/series/21debates/drugstrade

FACT

Between 1990 and 2000, seizures of ATS grew at an average annual rate of 28 per cent, compared to 8 per cent for heroin, 6 per cent for cannabis herb, 5 per cent for cannabis resin, and 1.5 per cent for cocaine.

A drug user lights a marijuana cigarette (usually called a joint or reefer) made from the dried leaves and flowering tops of the cannabis plant, mixed with tobacco.

Cocaine

Cocaine comes from the leaves of the coca bush, widely grown in South America. It is refined into a white powder that is usually snorted up the nose. Crack is a form of cocaine, made into small lumps or 'rocks', which can be smoked and can also be prepared for injection. Cocaine is a stimulant that causes a feeling of exhilaration and decreases appetite. Users often feel positive, confident and energetic, and indifferent to pain and tiredness. However, after the effects wear off, they may feel anxious and depressed, as well as very hungry or tired. Regular snorting of the drug can damage the membranes of the nose, and injection carries a risk of infection from HIV and hepatitis through the use of shared needles. Cocaine is not physically addictive but users may come to depend on it and so go on to use more of it. Long-term use can make people anxious and paranoid. Excessive doses can cause death from respiratory or heart failure, although this is rare.

Ecstasy

Ecstasy is an illegally manufactured, synthetic drug that usually comes in tablet form. The tablets are swallowed and are popular among young people on the dance or club scene. Ecstasy is partly derived from a type of amphetamine. Most users say it causes a sense of euphoria (extreme happiness), followed by a sense of calm. However, some people say that ecstasy has made them feel panicky or confused, with a disturbing heightening of their senses. Ecstasy affects body temperature and, when combined with dancing for long periods in hot places, users can risk dehydration which may be fatal (there have been well reported deaths of teenagers who have taken ecstasy). After taking ecstasy, users may feel very low and tired and need a long time to recover from the experience. Little is known at present about the effects of long-term use; it is thought that the drug may cause brain damage and mental illness.

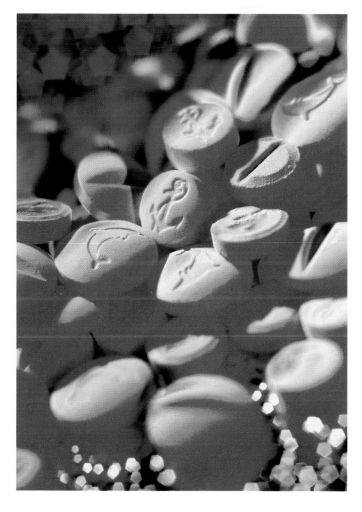

Ecstasy pills with designs on them which assure users of their quality.

Tranquillizers

Minor tranquillizers are mainly used as medicines to treat anxiety and sleeping problems (major tranquillizers are used to treat long-term mental health problems). Tranquillizers are usually swallowed as pills or capsules but some forms can also be prepared for injection. In recent years prescribed or stolen tablets have found their way on to the street market. They are only really effective as short-term medicines but many people take them for several years. A lot of people have died from taking a combination of tranquillizers and alcohol.

VIEWPOINTS

'I watched a play at school recently about drugs, telling us how it can affect your life. It made me realize how stupid drugs are and how people can waste their lives taking them. We are always being given stuff at school asking us what we think about drugs, which I think is a good thing.'
Jamie. UK

'Anyone who is shocked when they hear about kids smoking cannabis is kidding themselves. Many of my friends do it, and it's not just cannabis either – they take harder drugs. I don't want to get involved – but I know a lot of young people who are.'
David. USA

Heroin

Heroin is one of a group of drugs called 'opiates', derived from the opium poppy. Opium is the dried 'milk' extracted from the poppy seed head and contains morphine, a powerful painkiller. Heroin is refined from morphine. In its pure form it is a white or brown powder that can be smoked, sniffed or injected. Heroin and other opiates are sedative drugs that depress the nervous system. They slow down body functioning and can reduce physical pain and emotional distress. Heroin users often experience a feeling of well-being, contentment and detachment from normal worries. However, sharing needles can increase the risk of infection with diseases such as HIV and hepatitis. Tolerance builds up very quickly so that ever-greater amounts of the drug are needed to create 'a high'. This quickly leads to physical addiction and increases the risk of overdose. Withdrawal after regular use can produce flu-like symptoms and may include aches, tremors, sweating, chills and muscular spasms. Heroin can cause death because the user has a particular reaction to the drug, or to injecting heroin, or to impurities present in the drug. Long-term effects include collapsed veins, loss of appetite and severe constipation.

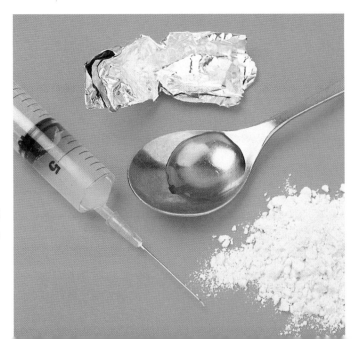

Equipment used by a heroin addict, including a hypodermic syringe, and heroin powder which is dissolved in water before being injected.

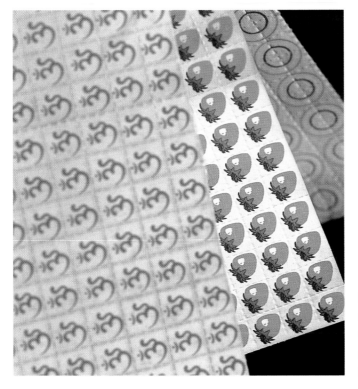

Sheets of blotting paper cut into squares (or tabs) and soaked with LSD. Different 'brands' of LSD are identified by the illustration on each tab.

LSD

LSD was originally derived from the ergot fungus which grows on rye and other grasses. It can now be manufactured artificially and is usually sold as a liquid, either on its own or soaked on to squares of blotting paper. LSD is also sometimes put onto sugar cubes or formed into tablets or small capsules. It was used in the 1960s by several writers and intellectuals who thought that it heightened their creativity. It is still popular today. LSD is a hallucinogenic drug. Users experience a heightened visual sense, with objects seeming much brighter and perhaps appearing to move or change shape. Many users have frightening or disturbing 'trips'. They do not become physically dependent on LSD – but may become psychologically dependent, sometimes experiencing distressing flashbacks. LSD has been linked with long-term psychiatric illnesses, such as schizophrenia.

PRODUCTION OF ILLEGAL DRUGS

FACT

The United Nations Drug Control Programme (UNDCP) estimates that Afghanistan produced nearly 80 per cent of all the world's opium in 1999, and Colombia more than 65 per cent of unprocessed coca.

Many illegal drugs originate in developing countries in Asia and South America. However the refined drugs will mostly be sold in developed countries such as the USA and the UK. Coca, for instance, is grown in Colombia, Peru and Bolivia, and opium in Afghanistan, while the refined drugs (cocaine and heroin) are usually 'trafficked' on to developed countries. At the same time, the developed world is becoming a significant producer of cannabis as well as synthetic drugs (such as ecstasy and amphetamines). Some synthetic drugs produced in developed countries are now also transported to growing markets in South-East Asia.

Why do farmers in the developing world grow illegal drug crops?

Many poor farmers in developing countries grow drug-related crops because it is the only way for them to make a living and to feed their families. In most cases the only alternative would be to produce cash crops, such as coffee, bananas or pineapples, for export to wealthier countries. However, growing food for sale abroad raises a number of problems for poor farmers. Poor-quality soils and lack of fertilizers may make it difficult to grow these crops; the price they can sell them for is often very low because many other farmers are producing the same crops; and food products, such as fruit, may be delicate and bulky and difficult to transport to market.

In contrast, the production of drug-related crops is often much more profitable. Coca, for example, will grow quickly on very poor, exhausted soils that

weblinks

For an interactive guide to drug producing countries go to www.waylinks.co.uk/series/21debates/drugstrade

will not support other crops, avoiding the need for expensive fertilizers. It is also a crop which cannot be grown in developed countries (largely because it is illegal) but for which there is great demand, so that farmers get a better price for what they have grown. The problems of transporting goods to market are often solved by 'middle-men' who buy the crop, process it, and sell it on at a considerable profit. It is these people who make the most money from the drugs trade. Poor farmers would often prefer to grow other, legal crops, but feel that they have little or no alternative.

Young Peruvian girls harvest coca leaves.

The control of drug-related crop production is frequently in the hands of criminal groups, or anti-government forces, who may sell the drugs in order to fund and support their activities. For instance, anti-government guerrillas, such as the Revolutionary Armed Forces of Colombia (FARC), have been associated with coca production and trafficking, and the Wa rebels in Myanmar with the production of opium. It is also clear that some governments 'tax' and benefit from the drugs trade, even while officially condemning it. The involvement of anti-government groups in the production of illegal drugs, and the fact that some governments tolerate the drugs trade, leads to a great deal of instability, violence and conflict in some developing countries.

Opium production
The so-called 'Golden Crescent' (Afghanistan, Iran and Pakistan) is a significant base for the illicit production of poppies, from which opium is extracted and heroin is refined. Afghanistan has the largest opium industry in the world, while Pakistan has until recently been a significant producer, and Iran is the country through which much heroin is brought into Europe.

The Golden Crescent area's hot, dry conditions make it difficult to grow many food crops for export or even for local consumption, but they are ideally suited to poppy farming which takes much less water, and can earn farmers much more money. For instance, a peasant farmer in Afghanistan, who grows opium rather than grain, can earn as much as $13,000 (instead of $100) for a season's crops.

Each spring in Afghanistan, huge areas of the south and east of the country are covered with red opium poppies. Weeks later, after the flowers have seeded, farmers make holes in the seed heads and scrape off the white, milky liquid (opium). Some of it is processed into heroin inside Afghanistan, but much of it is sold unprocessed and is sent to 'factories' in Pakistan and Central Asia for refinement.

The former Taliban government (which fell in late 2001) officially banned opium production in 2000, and much less was therefore produced in 2001. However, the terrorist attacks on America on 11 September 2001, and the subsequent fall of the Taliban, coincided with the poppy planting season and new crops were grown at this time.

Members of the Taliban destroy poppy fields in eastern Afghanistan in 2000. As Islamic fundamentalists, the Taliban were opposed to drug-taking. Their action was also partly in response to pressure from the international community.

VIEWPOINT

'We realize the harm
this stuff does around
the world but I have
kids. How will they
survive? I'd love to get
out of it. I used to
raise fish.... I made
really good money out
of it. But then my
neighbour started
putting fish in ponds...
There was too much
fish and no-one wanted
to buy it anymore.
Unless the government
can guarantee that
someone is going to
buy what we grow, we
can't survive.'
Felix, coca farmer, Colombia

Although the Afghan Interim Administration issued a new ban on 17 January 2002, farmers had already planted poppies and production rose in 2002. Farmers sell raw opium for about $50 a kilo but by the time it is sold (as heroin) on the streets of London or New York, for instance, the price is likely to be up to 2000 times higher.

The other major area where opium is produced is 'the Golden Triangle' (Myanmar, Laos and Thailand). Myanmar, formerly known as Burma, is the second largest producer of opium and heroin after Afghanistan, growing about 15 per cent of the world's supply. In Myanmar, much of the opium industry is in the hands of anti-government rebels, and the government claims that it has no control over these rebels. In fact, the government has granted autonomy (the right to control a particular area without reference to the official government of the country) to the Wa, a rebel group living in the opium-growing area near the Chinese border, implying a certain amount of official acceptance of the trade. Laos is the most significant producer of opium after Myanmar, although its output is much smaller. Thailand has been a major producer in the past but improved standards of living in the country mean that there is less reason for people to rely on it for their livelihood, and production for export has almost stopped.

Coca production

Coca has long been an important part of cultural and social life in the Andean countries of South America (Colombia, Bolivia and Peru). The people here chew coca leaves as part of everyday life, and also use it for religious ceremonies and medicinal purposes. The coca plant is now, however, also widely grown for export and the manufacture of cocaine. The Andean countries, supported and financed by the USA, have made some serious attempts to reduce the production of coca in the area – but when production falls in one country or region, it typically increases in another so that the supply remains relatively constant.

In the 1990s Colombia was mainly the base for refining coca grown in Bolivia and Peru, but by 1997 it had become the world's largest producer. Colombia is now also a leading supplier of opium to the United States. During most of the 1990s Peru was the world's major producer of coca but now produces much less than before.

Two workers on a small farm in southern Colombia mix coca leaves with cement in the first stage of making cocaine base. The base is then refined to make pure cocaine. About 570 kg of leaves make 1 kg of base which makes a little less than 1 kg of pure cocaine.

FACT

Some people say coca is a major cause of deforestation in the Andes as forest is cleared for land to grow it on. Other sources say that, as coca can grow on soil too exhausted to support other crops and is farmed less intensively, it is better for the environment than legal alternatives.

Bolivia is the world's third largest producer of coca, though output is in steep decline, and the government aims to get rid of illicit coca production entirely. Large areas of the crop have been destroyed in the main coca-growing area, Chapare, under the government's Dignity Plan. This caused a great deal of hardship and suffering to poor farmers who have had their livelihoods destroyed (see pages 46-47).

Many people question whether eliminating the production of drug-related crops is the right way to tackle the problem. Destroying crops destroys the living of poor farmers and, as the experience of the Andes has shown, if there is still a demand for drugs from developed countries – the crops will only be grown elsewhere.

In 1995 drug squad detectives raided a basement in Manchester, UK, and discovered a £1 million pound haul of cannabis.

Cannabis

Cannabis is by far the most widely cultivated illegal drug and is grown in many more countries than any other drug-related crop. In fact the United Nations Office for Drug Control and Crime Prevention (UNODCCP) states that it grows in at least two-thirds of all countries in the world, compared to 20 per cent of countries for opium poppies, and 4 per cent for coca.

Morocco, Afghanistan and Pakistan are by far the most important sources of cannabis resin, while Mexico, Colombia, Jamaica and Thailand are significant producers of herbal cannabis (or marijuana) for the North American market. Many small farmers in developing countries, such as Jamaica, rely on the production of cannabis for export for a living. However, cannabis is also starting to be cultivated in developed countries. Now, up to 50 per cent of the Netherlands' cannabis is grown locally, and between 20 and 50 per cent of the American cannabis supply is grown in the United States, hidden in homes, gardens and wasteland areas.

Synthetic drugs

Unlike the plant-based drugs discussed above, the consumption of synthetic drugs is growing rapidly and many people believe that the most significant drugs problems of the future will be associated with them. The Netherlands is a major producer of synthetic drugs, such as amphetamines and ecstasy, and most of the ecstasy available in Europe is manufactured in either the Netherlands or Poland. South-East Asia provides a growing market for ecstasy produced in Europe, a reversal of the Asia–Europe distribution pattern that has traditionally applied to illegal drugs such as cannabis and heroin.

VIEWPOINT

'I grow coca because the price of coffee is so low. If I grow coffee I cannot cover my costs, I cannot make a living and I cannot feed my family. The price I get for my coca is much higher and means I can afford to live.'
Pedro, Peru

DEBATE

Why do poor farmers in developing countries decide to grow illegal drug crops? Do you think they are right to do so? Do you think that they have any real alternatives?

TRAFFIC!

The trafficking of illegal drugs is a multimillion-dollar global activity – and the enforcement of international drugs laws to combat it also uses up vast resources. Yet customs officials and police officers in the developed world agree that only about 10 per cent of illegal drugs are ever intercepted. In 2002 the UK adopted a less strict policy on 'soft drugs' (such as cannabis and LSD) in order to free more resources to concentrate on the seizure of 'hard drugs' (such as heroin and cocaine) – in an effort to ensure that more are captured and that the supply is stemmed.

Colombian police seized more than 500 kg of cocaine that was being smuggled to the USA in suitcases on an Avianca Airlines flight in 1994.

Drug trafficking involves a range of people, from powerful drugs barons who control the trade and derive most of the benefit, to individual couriers who carry parcels of drugs into other countries. Like the poor farmers who grow drug-related crops, the couriers usually become involved because they need the money. Drug trafficking brings great wealth to the powerful groups who control it, fuelling violence and corruption and undermining legal governments. For individuals caught up in the trade it may seem like an economic lifeline, although it actually offers them a very risky, short-term, insecure livelihood.

With increasing globalization, the trafficking of drugs from producers to consumers is becoming ever more complex and sophisticated. The removal of border controls in Europe, the ease with which it is possible to move money (including 'dirty money', derived from crime) from country to country, and the ease of global communications, have all led to a growth in trafficking. The UN's World Drug Report 2000 states that the number of countries involved in trafficking has risen from 120 in the early 1980s to 170 in the late 1990s. There are a number of traditional routes through which drugs are moved:

- Cocaine is usually trafficked from the Andean countries of South America to North America and Europe, either directly, or through Mexico and the Caribbean.

- Opiates are trafficked from Afghanistan via Pakistan, Iran, Turkey and the Balkans (or, increasingly, Central Asia) to Europe. Now Colombian opium is also trafficked along traditional cocaine routes from the Andes to the USA, and from Myanmar to China.

VIEWPOINT

'International drug law enforcement is a victim of its own success because we did know a lot about the major cartels [in South America]... Today ... it's so much more diverse. So yeah, it's a problem.'
Mark Eissler. Head of Intelligence. DEA. Washington. USA

- Cannabis herb (or marijuana) is moved through Mexico to the USA, while cannabis resin is moved from Morocco via Spain and other European countries.

- Synthetic drugs are moved in a much more unpredictable way. They tend to be produced quite close to where they are consumed.

Cocaine from South America

Cocaine from South America has long been associated with high-profile drug cartels, such as the Cali and Medallin cartels in Colombia. These powerful groups have now lost some of their power, and smaller groups, whose activities are harder to detect, have taken control of the trade. Mexican drug groups, such as the Arellano Felix brothers, also play a big role in trafficking to the US, particularly in the southern and western states. Traffickers have links to criminal networks, such as the Mafia (in the USA and Italy), and organized crime groups in Russia. They are therefore involved in a whole web of illegal activities.

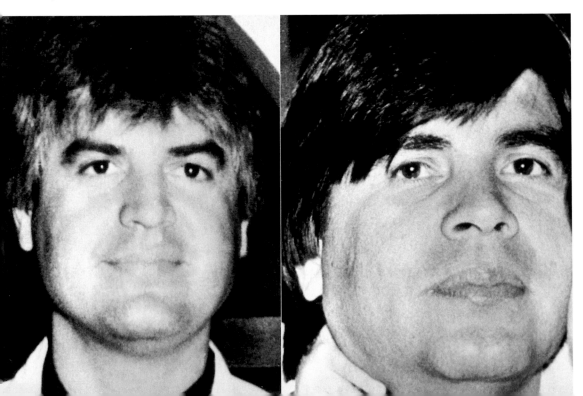

Ramon Arellano Felix, left, and his brother Benjamin, right, two of Mexico's most wanted drugs barons, in photos released in 1998.

French customs officers display almost 358,000 ecstasy tablets, seized at Calais in 1998. The drugs were hidden in a Belgian-registered lorry heading for Britain.

Consignments of cocaine tend to be quite bulky, making it reasonably easy to identify and to seize. Although the amount of cocaine produced worldwide is only twice that of opiates, five times more cocaine is intercepted by police, customs officers and international agents. Routes and methods of transport for trafficking are constantly changing and may involve air-drops, boats and individual couriers.

Cocaine from South America is often flown in small planes and dropped in Caribbean Islands such as Jamaica. Here it may be brought to the UK by a 'mule' (someone who swallows drugs, usually in a condom to stop them being digested, or hides them in their clothing, before boarding a normal passenger flight). The couriers who agree to do this are usually desperately poor, often single mothers with families to look after, for whom trafficking seems like the only available option. They are rarely greedy or corrupt. They are usually ordinary people who have fallen on hard times. Many will not be aware of the value of the drugs they carry and most will not be significant drug users themselves. They often do not even realize that they are committing a crime, or that they may be arrested and imprisoned.

FACT

The US/Mexican border, where the Arellano Felix brothers are active in drug trafficking, has seen a great deal of crime. Between 2001 and 2002 there were around 400 murders just in the town of Tijuana. Drug trafficking played a part in nearly every case.

Opiates from Asia

Heroin trafficking is concentrated in Asia, where most opium is produced. Iran is the main land route for opiates produced in Afghanistan. They tend to be taken overland by truck through Turkey and the Balkans for sale in Western Europe.

With international support, Iran has now launched a concerted attack on the traffickers. Along the country's eastern and western borders, an elaborate system of barbed wire fences and trenches aims to keep the traffickers out. There have been reports of traffickers blasting their way past border fortifications with machine guns, or using 'mules' – men and women who cross the border carrying heroin on their own bodies. Iran accounted for 47 per cent of the world's opiate seizures in 1999 – reflecting the government's strong enforcement of international drugs laws, as well as the extent of opium trafficking in the area.

Iran also illustrates another disturbing trend – the growth of opiate abuse along well-established trafficking routes: on average, 2.8 per cent of the Iranian population are now using opiates every year, a figure far higher than in western Europe. Opium use has long been common in the country but now it, and heroin use, is rising, particularly among young people experiencing

Veiled Iranian women watch as illegal drugs seized by Iranian authorities burn in northern Tehran. In 2000, Iran burned 23 tonnes of illegal drugs worth $3 billion, a measure of the problem facing a country that is used as a major transit route.

social problems such as unemployment and a high cost of living. One young Iranian said in an interview, 'Opium gives me relief from the stress and tension I feel in my life. It is also medicine, and in this sense it is a medicine for me…' All over the world, drug use is rising in areas around trafficking routes.

An Iranian soldier leads away camels seized on the border between Iran and Afghanistan. Smugglers use unmanned camels to transport opium through the desert to central Iran, in order to avoid being arrested themselves. The smugglers recapture the animals on the other side of the border, before taking the opium on to Europe by vehicle.

Cannabis

Cannabis is the most widely consumed drug in the world, and also the most widely trafficked. The most significant drug seizures made are cannabis-related, accounting for half of all seizures (in terms of volume and number of cases). Morocco is one of the largest producers and traffickers of cannabis, and cannabis resin is taken via Spain to Europe. Cannabis herb tends to be taken from Colombia and Jamaica, through Mexico, to the USA.

Synthetic drugs

Trafficking in synthetic drugs usually takes place within (rather than between) continents and regions, and areas of production tend to be close to the consumer market. Because synthetic drugs are not trafficked over long distances (like cannabis, cocaine and heroin) it is much rarer for them to be intercepted by drug enforcement agencies.

FACT

In Australia, in 2001, 17.5 per cent of people over the age of fifteen were using cannabis. In the UK, the figure was 9 per cent, and in the Netherlands it was 5.2 per cent.

VIEWPOINT

'Ten years ago there were no Nigerians in prison here, our lives were good – we didn't have to resort to drug dealing.... The gap between rich and poor is enormous. There is no hope if I don't do drug business, of ever breaking out of being poor ... that's why lots of us are taking this risk – we know if we are caught we'll go to jail, but how long can we live poor?'

Peter, a Nigerian, imprisoned for importing 190 g of heroin, quoted in Penny Green, Drugs, Trafficking and Criminal Policy, 1998

A Nigerian prisoner serves his sentence for drug smuggling in an overcrowded prison in Bangkok, Thailand.

Even so, trafficking in amphetamine-type stimulants (ATS) grew more quickly than any other drug category over the last decade, with seizures quadrupling during the 1990s. The trafficking of ATS has also become more organized and sophisticated since the 1990s and has been taken over by organized crime networks.

The unique role of Nigeria

A number of African countries, especially Nigeria, are now transit countries for drugs produced elsewhere. Nigeria plays a surprisingly significant role in the global drugs trade, even though it is not a large-scale producer. Since the early 1980s it has become known as an important centre for worldwide trafficking. Nigerian crime networks import Asian heroin into the US, and South American cocaine into Europe, Asia and Africa. Traditionally, individual couriers, who conceal drugs on their bodies, have been used, and hundreds of Nigerians are serving prison sentences in foreign jails for drug smuggling. But drugs are now more frequently transported in bigger quantities, hidden in lorry containers or the holds of ships.

US customs officers use a cutting torch to open a secret compartment on the keel of a Haitian cargo ship used to smuggle cocaine in 2000.

As with so many other countries, Nigeria's involvement in the drugs trade is largely due to its poverty. In 1985 it was one of the wealthiest nations in Africa, with a per capita (per person) income of US$1,200 a year. However Nigeria had built up a lot of debts, in the form of large development loans from banks in developed countries. When these debts had to be repaid, Nigeria's wealth soon changed to poverty. By 1991, per capita incomes had dropped to $250 and it was the thirteenth poorest country in Africa.

Money laundering

Another problem for national and international governments, closely linked to drug trafficking, is money laundering. Organized crime generates huge sums of money through the drug trade. The criminals must then 'launder' (or 'clean') this 'dirty money' in order to spend it without being detected. They do this by moving funds quickly across borders, particularly to those countries where legal controls are weak or non-existent. Once they have placed the money in new, secret bank accounts, it becomes very difficult for the authorities to trace its illegal origins. The UN's Global Programme Against Money Laundering is the international institution working to combat money laundering.

---

weblinks

For an interactive look at the countries involved in drug trafficking go to
www.waylinks.co.uk/series/
21debates/drugstrade

DEBATE

What effect do you think drug trafficking has on the countries where it takes place? Why do you think individuals become involved in the trade? Do you think they are ever justified in doing so?

WHO USES ILLEGAL DRUGS?

Many people might think of a 'typical drug user' as a heroin addict, perhaps homeless and unemployed, whose life is out of control and who is forced into crime in order to sustain his or her expensive habit. This is certainly true of some drug users, and heroin is particularly addictive and difficult to manage. However, in reality, drug users come from all walks of life. They may range from the young unemployed man stealing to support a habit, to the city lawyer taking recreational cocaine, to the middle-class working mother taking alcohol, cannabis or prescription drugs to help her cope with the pressures of life.

Finding out how many people use drugs is very difficult, as we need to measure the level of an activity that is usually hidden, and nearly always illegal. However, as we saw in Chapter 1, the United Nations Drug Control Programme estimates that more than 180 million people worldwide were using illegal drugs at the end of the 1990s. The British Crime Survey 2001 found that half of all young people in the UK aged sixteen to twenty-four have tried drugs at some point, and 18 per cent said they had used an illegal drug, mostly cannabis, in the previous month.

A homeless man injects heroin in London.

Drug use trends

Drug abuse is a global phenomenon experienced by countries throughout the world. Cannabis is the most widely used drug, but heroin and cocaine are generally thought to be the most problematic ones, in terms of addiction, treatment needs, and associated crime. Different regions of the world tend to experience problems with different drugs, according to patterns of production, trafficking and supply in that area. Opiates are the most significant drug problem in Europe, Asia, Australia and New Zealand; cocaine in North and South America; ATS in parts of East and South-East Asia; and cannabis in Africa. Levels of use of the most problematic drugs, including heroin and cocaine, are now fairly stable in Western Europe and the USA. Perhaps surprisingly, however, use of these drugs is rising steeply in many 'producer' countries in the developing world.

A young woman smoking cannabis.

VIEWPOINT

'You can get addicted pretty quickly and start feeling you have to have it all the time. It's cut with all sorts of rubbish but you don't really care. The only goal in life became getting more. It kind of took all my feelings away.'
Heroin user, quoted on the DrugScope website

A father and his son at work in their poppy field in eastern Afghanistan in 1992. The opium they produce is increasingly being used by young Afghanis.

Afghanistan, while the most significant producer of opium, has not until recently been a major consumer, and the Taliban government had a strict policy against drug use. Now more people in Afghanistan are using opium themselves: the increasing numbers of heroin factories and abandoned needles show that heroin is more widely available and is being injected. Myanmar has one of the most serious HIV epidemics in Asia, with over half a million people HIV positive in 1999, partly due to the country's problem with injected heroin. Cocaine use (rather than the traditional chewing of coca leaves) is also growing in a number of South American countries.

Why do people take drugs?

Today most of us realize that all legal and illegal drug use, no matter how limited, carries some immediate risk and may also cause longer-term harm. So why do people from all walks of life expose themselves to these dangers? There are a number of factors, including:

- Environmental factors – people may be influenced to take drugs because of the experiences they are having at the time, or the group of people they are with.

- Psychological factors – for example, low self-esteem may make people particularly susceptible to drugs.

- Genetic factors – some people may be naturally more inclined to use, abuse, and become addicted to drugs, including alcohol and tobacco, than others.

Some people also use drugs for medical reasons. For instance, sufferers from multiple sclerosis may use cannabis to manage their pain, and there is a

FACT

In July 2001 Canada became the first country in the world to legalize the use of cannabis for medicinal purposes, allowing those with chronic and terminal illnesses to grow and use their own.

growing feeling (in Great Britain, supported by the British Medical Association) that such use should be officially permitted.

Environmental factors

Teenagers often use drugs because they are pleasurable or exciting or in order to overcome feelings of shyness and lack of confidence. They may also take drugs because it makes them feel sophisticated or rebellious. Leaving home, perhaps to go away to work or university, can provide new freedom from the constraints of family life – and thus a greater opportunity or temptation to take illegal drugs. People experiencing certain social problems, such as unemployment, poverty, abusive parents or single parenthood, may also turn to drugs, thinking that they will help them cope with these difficulties.

A village head and a trader weigh some opium in Shan State, Myanmar.

Psychological factors

However, the question remains: what makes one teenager or person experiencing social problems more likely to take drugs than another? Here, psychological factors may come into play. Certain personal attributes may make some young people more likely to experiment with drugs than others. A tendency to engage in other 'risky' activities (such as drinking or smoking) and, most crucially, poor self-esteem and difficulty in resisting peer pressure, are all factors encouraging the use of drugs.

Genetic factors

Although it is a controversial theory, some scientists believe that people may be 'genetically inclined' to develop diseases such as alcoholism and drug addiction. Studies of twins separated at birth, or siblings who have been adopted by different families, suggest that genetics plays a significant role in the development of individuals and may be more important than family environment. These studies seem to show that certain types of alcoholism can be transmitted genetically.

This heroin user, seen in a London hostel, is HIV positive, probably due to his use of injected drugs.

The consequences

Although there is an assumption that illegal drug use is extremely dangerous and a significant cause of death among young people, in fact cigarettes cause the deaths of far more people in Britain than heroin, cocaine or alcohol. Many of the problems associated with 'hard' drug use relate to the circumstances in which the drugs are taken – poor injecting techniques (such as the use of dirty, shared needles), the association of drug use with crime, and taking adulterated street drugs (drugs which have been mixed with other, toxic substances), rather than the sheer fact of taking illegal drugs.

It is also very important to make a distinction between drug use and drug addiction. Experimentation with soft drugs does not necessarily mean that the user will go on to take hard drugs, and the use of hard drugs does not inevitably lead to addiction. Although very addictive, it is possible for some people to take both heroin and cocaine on an occasional basis, although even rare usage may be risky or fatal. Some people talk about 'visible' and 'invisible' drug use, as most drug users will never come to the attention of doctors, police or lawyers. These people manage their habit themselves, albeit sometimes at great cost to their own lives.

VIEWPOINT

'It doesn't seem like a big deal. I often smoke a joint after dinner. It helps me to relax and take away the stresses of work. The next day I feel fine.'
Cannabis user, Edinburgh, Scotland

A successful businessman copes with his stressful job during the day and may occasionally choose to use soft drugs for relaxation in the evening.

However, even short-term drug-taking can be dangerous and habitual hard drug use can certainly destroy lives. For example, 'Johnnie' began taking heroin occasionally with friends to help him cope with family problems. When he began to take it more frequently he lost a job he had enjoyed and ended up stealing from his family to support his habit. He lost contact with other friends and eventually contracted hepatitis C, a serious disease. With support he has now overcome his addiction, and has a new job and a new group of friends. Other drug users may not be so lucky.

This young girl's feelings of depression and insecurity could make her more vulnerable to the dangers of drugs.

Drug use around the world

In New York, an intense police campaign against users of crack cocaine has succeeded in stabilizing cocaine use. Heroin abuse is increasing, however, and ecstasy use is also widespread and rising. Seizures of ecstasy in the first half of 2000 far exceeded those for the whole of 1999 – a 'phenomenal increase', according to US Customs.

In London, drugs are an integral part of the capital's nightlife and ecstasy is widely used by young people wanting to dance all night. Cocaine use is still rising, perhaps partly because the US market seems saturated and traffickers are turning their attention more to Europe. The use of amphetamines is also widespread.

Meanwhile, in parts of Asia, drug abuse is now a major problem. In Vietnam, despite concerted government efforts, it is rising steadily, especially among young people in the cities. The country produces some opium but it is also a transit country for heroin from 'the Golden Triangle', and synthetic drugs from China and Myanmar. Synthetic drugs are a growing problem in Vietnam, and many other Asian countries.

Back in the developed world, in Australia there were 1,000 drug-related deaths in 1998, most of them young people aged fifteen to thirty-four. In the same year, half of all Australians said that they had used an illegal drug at some stage in their lives, and about 1 per cent said they had recently used cocaine or heroin. Marijuana and synthetic drug use rose steeply in the 1990s.

At the other end of the scale, Denmark has a lower percentage of heroin abusers than the UK, Australia or the USA. As in most countries, cannabis is the most widely used drug.

weblinks

For more information about drugs and health go to www.waylinks.co.uk/series/21debates/drugstrade

DEBATE

Why do you think some people are able to deal with drug-taking better than others? Who could you talk to if you, or someone you know, had a problem with drugs? See the resources section of this book for some ideas.

LOOKING TOWARDS SOLUTIONS

VIEWPOINT

'The idea that the war against drugs and the international drugs trade can be won without tackling the issue of poverty is an illusion.'
Stan Newens MEP, talking at a Catholic Institute for International Relations (CIIR) seminar, 1998

Most people agree that the trade in illegal drugs is a global problem, but views differ sharply as to the best way of tackling it. This chapter looks specifically at the ways in which countries and institutions have attempted to reduce the supply of illegal drugs, by stopping the production of drug-related crops, particularly in developing countries.

Two quite distinct strategies are being adopted on this issue – the aggressive 'war on drugs' approach, and the more co-operative alternative development approach. The USA, for instance, has tended to emphasize the need for a war on drugs and has provided funding for governments in developing countries to destroy drug crops, in order to stop the trade. The alternative development approach, however, recognizes that the problem is linked to poverty in the developing world, and demand in the developed world, and that any solution must address both these issues.

The US 'war on drugs'
On 5 September 1989 President George Bush Senior responded to the failure of US drug policy until then by declaring a 'war on drugs'. The principal weapons in such a war would be the enforcement of international drug laws and the

In 1998, Randy Beers, centre, then US Assistant Secretary of State for Narcotics and International Crime, went on a fact-finding mission to Colombia to find out about its anti-drug efforts. In the background, Colombian police have set fire to a small building used to process coca leaves into cocaine base.

destruction of drug-related crops. In the Andes, the US has been fighting this war aggressively for some time. The US has provided financial and military support to the governments of Colombia, Peru and Bolivia to destroy drug crops and fight anti-government 'narco-guerrillas' associated with their production. The USA has also given substantial funding to the Colombian government, under its Plan Colombia, to fight the FARC guerrillas who are associated with drug production and trafficking. Many people would say, however, that the USA has another agenda: that the 'war on drugs' is an excuse for the USA to provide military support to the Colombian government in order to fight the left-wing guerrillas who oppose it.

VIEWPOINT

'The time has come to change the way we think about drugs. The World Community must end the psychology of despair that has gripped the minds of a generation and instead focus on a pragmatic, long-term approach to reducing both the supply of, and demand for, illicit drugs.'
Pino Arlacchi, Executive Director, the United Nations Office for Drug Control and Crime Prevention (ODCCP)

A FARC Communist guerrilla in Colombia, 1992.

A Colombian police plane sprays glyphosate on a coca plantation in 1996, 250 km southeast of Bogota.

Chemical fumigation has also been a part of US-backed crop eradication plans in the Andes. Aerial spraying of herbicides has been used to destroy huge areas of coca. But there is grave concern about the effect of this spraying on people's health and livestock, and on the sensitive ecosystem of the Amazon rainforest.

Crops, chickens and fish have been destroyed, and the local people have experienced breathing problems, skin infections and stomach pains. Health and safety warnings attached to the chemical sprays are frequently ignored. And even after spraying, the coca can often be saved, by cutting off the leaves to prevent the chemicals reaching the roots. In any case, this hardy crop is usually simply then planted elsewhere. In 2001 a report in a British newspaper, the *Observer*, quoted Luis Fernando Arango, a Colombian lawyer and teacher, who opposed the spraying: 'Anyone who protests about this is labelled a drug dealer. Years in the future a lot of old men … will get together and talk about it. By then there will be no countryside left.'

In any case eradication does not work. Destruction of crops has been outpaced by new cultivation, because of the so-called 'balloon effect': crops are destroyed in one place, but are quickly planted by poor peasants in another, ensuring a continued supply. When drug-related crops are destroyed, the

weblinks

To read an article about the effects of chemical spraying of coca in the Andes go to
www.waylinks.co.uk/series/
21debates/drugstrade

A Colombian anti-narcotics police conscript, armed with a machine gun, secures a heroin poppy field, before spraying it with a defoliant, while the farmer and his young family look on. 'Operation Radiance', a US-funded campaign to eradicate this species of heroin poppy, as part of Washington's war on drugs, began in 1995.

poor farmers who grow them have no alternative way of making a living and may well resort to growing them again.

Alternative development

An alternative to the US war on drugs is the 'alternative development' approach, sponsored by the UN and favoured by the European Community. This approach aims to reduce the production of drug-related crops by promoting legal alternatives (such as food crops) that can provide an adequate livelihood for farmers in developing countries. UNDCP alternative-development programmes are being implemented in Latin America, South-West Asia and South-East Asia.

> ## VIEWPOINT
>
> 'I had just arrived from Cochamba when they told me soldiers were cutting my coca. I asked them to stop, but they didn't listen. Some were eating my pineapples, others were taking the oranges from my trees. They beat me.'
> *A farmer, Bolivia*

FACT

At a special session of the UN General Assembly on Drugs in 1998, 185 states agreed that all countries should work for a 50 per cent reduction in illegal drug consumption by 2008. In addition, those states where illegal production has taken place agreed to eliminate production by 2008, mainly by promoting the substitution (alternative development) of other, legal, crops.

Alternative development programmes should aim to involve the whole community in planning, to ensure that projects are based on local knowledge, skills, interests and needs – rather than on what an outsider may think will work for a particular village or community. The design of the projects should also include a 'gender perspective', consulting and involving women, who are so often responsible for a family's welfare.

Alternative development not only looks at switching from drug crops to legal alternatives but also aims to provide the technical, social and financial support that farmers will need to make sure that these changes succeed. Wider issues, such as the health and education needs of the community, are also considered. In 1998 a UN Special Assembly on drugs agreed the goal of eliminating illegal drug production by 2008, using alternative development as the key approach.

Difficulties with the alternative development approach

Even the alternative development approach has difficulties, however. Legal crops, such as cocoa beans, pineapples, bananas or coffee, which may replace coca, opium or cannabis are often much harder to grow, and certainly earn less for the farmers. Those promoting alternative development programmes cannot influence international markets for export crops, which are controlled by powerful multinational companies. Thus the price farmers get paid for their produce is often too low for them to make a living. And, all too often, communities feel that alternative development programmes are forced on them by overpaid 'outsiders', who do not really understand the many problems they face.

weblinks

For more information about the UN's alternative development approach go to
www.waylinks.co.uk/series/
21debates/drugstrade

The UN's 2008 target for the eradication of drug-related production has also been criticized. Some people feel that it is over-ambitious and will inevitably lead to lack of respect for human rights, failure to involve local people, and damage to the environment during crop eradication. Countries such as Thailand and Turkey have only been able to reduce illegal drug production when the economic condition of the whole country improved – independently of any drug control policies. In both cases worldwide opium supply did not decrease, however. Production simply moved to Afghanistan and Myanmar.

Peruvian farmers, who have switched from producing coca, check the quality of their cocoa plants.

Bolivia: The Dignity Plan

In Bolivia, the Dignity Plan aims to eliminate all illegal coca production, and to establish an alternative way for families to make a living. Coca growing has provided a living for 35,000 peasants in the Chapare region of Bolivia for twenty years. According to development agencies such as the Catholic Institute for International Relations (CIIR), violence and intimidation have been used to implement the ban on coca, and the farmers' livelihoods have been destroyed.

Armed police raid Bolivian coca farmers and impound the paste they have been making from coca leaves.

Alternative development schemes, such as cattle ranching and tourism, have been inappropriate for local conditions and have failed. Men have left the area to find paid work and only women have stayed behind, looking after children and growing basic foodstuffs for their own needs. Meanwhile, coca production has been moved to Colombia and, regionally, production has not decreased at all.

Angel is a Bolivian coca grower with a wife and four children. In 1990 he decided to stop growing coca and join an alternative development project to rear pigs. The pig rearing was not a success, however, and at the end of the year Angel and the other participants found themselves with nothing – no coca, no pigs, no money and no income. Angel started again. In 1992 he tried to take advantage of the boom in the pineapple market and took out a loan for US$700 to buy pineapple seedlings. Within two years the plants had been struck by disease and he lost everything. He could not even sell all the fruit that he had managed to harvest because the local market was saturated and he had no transport to get the fruit there. Now Angel believes he has no alternative and has resorted to planting coca again.

What is the solution?

It is very difficult to eliminate the production of drug-related crops. The economic realities mean that, once crops are destroyed, they will be planted and grown elsewhere, and the overall supply will not decrease. The most positive approach may be the alternative development path – but this needs to be combined with realistic prices and stable markets for cash crops. In any case, drug supply reduction in the developing world has to be combined with demand reduction in the developed world if it is to be effective.

VIEWPOINT

'We were lent money at 14 per cent interest. But then the interest rate went up ... and we had to pay off the loan at the new rate... We had to sell everything we had and we were still in debt. We lost everything.'
Felix, a Colombian coca grower, talking about borrowing money to develop alternative crops

VIEWPOINT

'Coca growers are not drugs traffickers.'
Veronica Ramos, Andean Information Network (AIN), talking at a CIIR seminar, 1998

DEBATE

How do you think poor farmers in developing countries could be enabled to stop growing drug-related crops?

WHAT ELSE CAN BE DONE?

As we have seen, an enormous amount of money is being spent on the prohibition of illegal drugs and the enforcement of international drugs laws. And yet the USA, which has one of the world's most repressive drugs policies, still has one of the most disturbing drugs problems. This shows that the issues raised by drugs are complex and hard to solve. It also suggests that reducing demand for drugs from the developed world may be more effective than trying to stop the supply.

In this chapter we look at different approaches to reducing the demand for drugs and helping drug users deal with their problems. We also consider whether the legalization or decriminalization of drugs might be more effective than prohibition.

Reducing the demand for drugs

There are a number of ways in which it may be possible to reduce demand for drugs in developed countries – firstly through education. For example, in the UK, the life of a 21-year-old former student, Rachel Whitear, who died in 2001 after injecting heroin, is now the focus of an education campaign warning schoolchildren of the dangers of drug abuse. Previous campaigns using images of dead drug users have not been particularly effective, however, and it is doubtful that such shock tactics really work.

The evidence suggests that appropriate education programmes can have a significant effect in reducing demand for drugs. But such programmes need to acknowledge the involvement young people may already have with drugs and provide accurate, non-sensational information about the effects of drug-taking. Some young people will already have experimented with drugs and they will know that occasional use does not make you an addict. They may also know that the effects of, say, cannabis and heroin are very different. While they realize that there are risks attached to drug-taking, their friends often put pressure on them to become involved. Education programmes that build on this realistic view have proved to be much more successful than those which take a 'drugs are evil' approach.

Strategies to promote young people's self-esteem are also important. With strong self-esteem, young people feel that they have control over their lives. They are more able to resist peer pressure, and less keen to risk their futures by taking part in activities that are likely to damage their health.

A drugs awareness lesson in a secondary school in Barnet, London.

Sandra and Carmen, two young Colombians, who are both prostitutes and drug addicts, on the streets of Bogota. Their drug abuse is the result of many different social problems which need to be tackled, including poverty, lack of family support and poor education.

VIEWPOINT

'As a parent I think the biggest problem this society has with drug taking is that the realities, effects and risks associated with taking drugs aren't openly discussed. Drug taking needs to be demystified so that parents are able to talk openly with their kids and kids talk openly with their parents.'
Parent, UK

Apart from education, the other major strategy is to tackle the social problems that may drive some individuals to take drugs. Much of the demand for hard drugs, such as heroin and crack, is due to social problems in both developed and developing countries. Street children in shanty towns in Brazil or Colombia, for instance, may use drugs to help them cope with cold, hunger, loneliness and abuse. And poor people in inadequate housing in the UK or the USA may also turn to crack, heroin or other drugs. Dealing with long-term social problems, such as unemployment and lack of housing, may be complex and expensive. But in the long run it will probably be cheaper, and more effective, than continuing to put vast resources into enforcing the prohibition of drugs.

Helping drug users

Another strategy to limit the harm done by drugs is to realistically acknowledge that drug-taking exists, and to manage it in the most appropriate way. Many of the problems associated with hard drug use are not due to the drugs themselves, but to the fact that they are illegal and people cannot get clean needles, health advice, and help when things go wrong. Syringe exchange schemes, health counselling of addicts, and even safe places in which to take drugs, can all limit the negative effects of drug-taking. In the Netherlands, harm reduction has been the principal approach used. Safe spaces have been provided, in which drugs such as heroin can be taken, needle exchange is routine, and drugs are seen as a social problem rather than a criminal activity. In the UK and USA, needle exchange schemes have also been promoted to limit the spread of HIV and AIDS.

There is also the issue of treatment for drug users, which raises a number of questions. What type of treatment works best? And how do we measure the effectiveness of a particular treatment? Is it only judged to be successful if the user gives up illegal drugs completely, as opposed to reducing their consumption and learning how to manage their drug-taking?

FACT

Six government-funded studies of HIV infection among drug users in the USA concluded that needle exchange programmes significantly reduced new HIV infections without encouraging drug use.

VIEWPOINT

'Take away the lies and the real danger becomes clear – not the drugs but the black market which has been created directly by the policy of prohibition.... There is no drug known to man which becomes safer when its production and distribution are handed over to criminals.'
Nick Davies, writing in the Guardian *newspaper, UK*

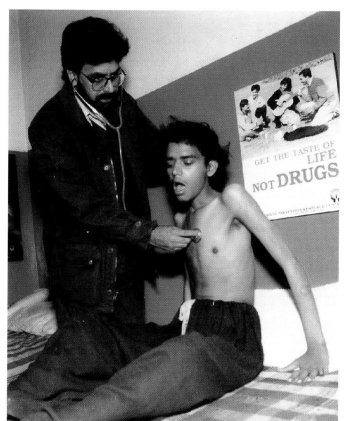

A Pakistani doctor examines a twenty-year-old heroin addict at a drug rehabilitation centre in Rawalpindi.

VIEWPOINTS

'Once you start talking about legitimising the use of cannabis, you are sending out a signal to young people that it's an OK thing to do.'
Anne Widdecombe MP, Health House, Channel 4 website

'I say legalise drugs because I want to see less drug abuse, not more. And I say legalise drugs because I want to see the criminals put out of business.'
Edward Ellison, former head of the Scotland Yard Drug Squad, Health House, Channel 4 website

Different approaches will work best for different individuals. And programmes which also look at other problems that users may face – such as poverty, homelessness and lack of support – are likely to be the most effective in the long term. Certain types of psychotherapy, which attempt to tackle negative patterns of thought, have been particularly successful in tackling drug use. And there are a range of other approaches offering help to drug users and their families.

The UN's World Drug Report 2001 claims that treatment of serious drug users is a successful strategy. Studies in the UK found that, two years after completing a treatment programme, a typical individual's heroin use and criminal activity were reduced by 50 per cent. Meanwhile, in the United States, one year after the end of treatment of drug addicts, their weekly heroin and cocaine use were down by two-thirds. However, drug treatment programmes are expensive and there are limited places available.

The legalization debate
Some commentators have argued that legalization of drugs is 'unthinkable'. To allow the use of dangerous, addictive substances that can impair quality of life, and even kill, seems unwise – at the very least. However, others argue that prohibition is not reducing drug use, and that the controlled use of drugs, regulated by the appropriate authorities, would be better.

Decriminalization is a halfway house between prohibition and legalization. The use of drugs is not legally sanctioned, but no action would be taken against anyone found carrying such drugs for their own use. However, people found selling such drugs to others would still be charged by the police.

Those in favour of legalization of drugs point out that their illegality ensures that drug trafficking and selling is kept entirely in the hands of criminals, with all the violence and corruption that this involves. It means that users are forced to come into contact with criminals in order to buy drugs – and dealers are likely to use abusive methods to push them to take more drugs more frequently, and to move on to harder drugs.

It also ensures that the enormous profits of the drugs trade stay in the hands of organized crime. If drugs were legalized, these profits could provide governments with money to spend on some of the social problems which fuel the drugs trade, as well as reducing the amount spent on enforcement of anti-drugs laws.

Police arrest a group of drug dealers in London.

VIEWPOINT

'There is no war on drugs in the Netherlands. What is the point of making war on part of your own country? Drugs are here and they're always going to be. This is a social problem, not a criminal one.'
Michael Vewer, senior police detective in the Netherlands, talking in the Guardian newspaper, UK, 2002

Those who are opposed to legalization say that it would only encourage more people to take drugs. At the moment the sheer fact of their illegality will put off many people who wish to stay within the law. It is also the most powerful signal a society can give to show that it does not approve of drug-taking.

Drugs laws around the world

In the USA the Drug Enforcement Agency (DEA) is strongly opposed to any softening of the drugs laws. Illegality, the DEA feels, is the best way of indicating that drug use is unacceptable.

In Britain the Runciman report suggested reducing penalties for the possession of some drugs including LSD and cannabis. A pilot project to decriminalize the use of soft drugs in Lambeth, London, was launched in July 2001. However there is some evidence that this policy has made all drugs more easily available in the area.

Portugal has decriminalized all previously banned narcotics, from cannabis to crack cocaine, in an effort to tackle its drugs problem. The new law, which came into effect on 1 July 2001, treats drug abuse as a social and health problem rather than a criminal one.

Cannabis smokers in a coffee shop in Amsterdam.

In the Netherlands cannabis has been available in coffee shops since 1976. Heroin addiction is not a major problem in the Netherlands. Per head of population, Holland has perhaps a quarter of Britain's addicts. It also has significantly fewer cannabis smokers.

weblinks

For more information on the legalization debate go to www.waylinks.co.uk/series/21debates/drugstrade

The choices that these young people make about drugs will have a significant impact on their futures.

The future of the drugs trade

So what patterns are emerging in the global drugs trade? ATS use is continuing to rise. More countries involved in production and trafficking are experiencing serious addiction problems. And the levels of drug use in developed countries have created major social, economic and political problems.

But there are some reasons for optimism. Levels of heroin use in Western Europe, and opiate use in North America, have been relatively stable, and may have declined slightly. There is evidence that strong education programmes, based on young people's own knowledge and experience of drugs, can be very effective in encouraging a safe and appropriate attitude to drug use. And radical new approaches, such as those in Portugal, and the Lambeth experiment in London, may have some impact on drug usage. Nevertheless the global drugs problem should continue to concern us all – and influence the choices and decisions we make.

DEBATE

What do you think about the legalization or decriminalization of drugs? Is it the best way to deal with the problems associated with illegal drugs? Or would it just encourage people to take more of them? Find out more about both sides of the argument. What do you think is the best way to tackle the 'drugs problem'?

GLOSSARY

addiction drug use can lead to dependency or addiction. This can be either physical (where the body needs or craves a certain drug) or psychological (where use is such an important part of life that the user cannot do without it). Someone who is addicted may be using drugs every day and will find it very hard to stop.

adulterated drugs drugs which have other impure ingredients added to them.

Afghan Interim Administration this interim administration took over the government of Afghanistan on a temporary basis in December 2001. The administration governed for six months.

alternative development an approach which encourages farmers to switch from growing drug-related crops to producing other, legal crops and offers them financial and technical support to do so.

autonomy the right to control or govern a particular area without reference to the official government of the country.

cartel a group which tries to maintain sole control of a particular activity, e.g. drug trafficking.

cash crops crops (e.g. coffee, tea, bananas, tropical fruit) which are grown to earn money by being exported, rather than for the farmer's own family to eat.

courier someone who carries drugs along part of a drug trafficking route.

decriminalization a compromise between full legalization and prohibition. For example, possession of drugs for personal use would not be a criminal offence.

depressants (tranquillizers or 'downers') These drugs seem to slow everything down, including thoughts, speech and action.

developed countries a term used to describe the (generally) richer countries of the world, in regions such as North America, Europe and Australia. These countries are also sometimes known as the West.

developing countries a term used to describe the (generally) poorer countries of the world, in regions such as Africa, Latin America, and Asia. These countries are also sometimes known as the Third World.

development agencies agencies concerned with the social and economic development of poor or developing countries.

Dignity Plan the Bolivian government's official plan for the social and economic development of the country. The plan aimed to eradicate the production of coca by 2002.

dirty money money earned through illegal means (e.g. crime, including the drugs trade).

ecosystem a system of interacting organisms (plants and wildlife) in a particular habitat or area.

euphoria extreme happiness.

Revolutionary Armed Forces of Colombia (FARC) a guerrilla group opposed to the official government of Colombia.

globalization the way in which countries and regions around the world are increasingly interconnected, socially, economically, culturally and in many other ways.

guerrilla a member of a small, independently acting group, often fighting against the official government of its own country.

hallucinogen a drug, e.g. cannabis, which alters the way people see, hear and feel things, causing hallucinations and confusion.

hard drugs drugs such as cocaine or heroin which are generally believed to be much more dangerous than 'soft drugs' such as cannabis or LSD.

indigenous people the people who originally inhabited an area, region, or country, e.g. Aboriginal people in Australia, and Maoris in New Zealand.

intoxication a state of excitement or exhilaration in which someone loses their self-control.

legalization to make an activity legal, so that a person is not fined or imprisoned for engaging in that activity. Legalization of drugs would mean that the supply and possession of currently illegal drugs would be legally controlled in the same way that alcohol or tobacco are controlled in most countries.

money laundering the 'cleaning' of 'dirty' money (money gained through crime, such as the sale of drugs), by processing it through legal bank accounts.

narcotic drugs an opiate or opiate-like drug that makes the user insensitive to pain or induces unconsciousness.

opium a substance extracted from the opium poppy that can be eaten or smoked for pleasure or used in medicine as a painkiller; the raw ingredient from which heroin is refined.

organized crime large-scale crime, such as the trafficking and sale of illegal drugs, which is organized and run by criminal gangs rather than individuals.

Plan Colombia the Colombian government's strategic development plan.

prohibition the banning, by law, of the sale or use of certain substances, in this case 'illegal' drugs.

psychotropic substance a drug that acts on the central nervous system, changing the way you think, feel and experience the world, e.g. LSD.

Qur'an the sacred book of Islam which contains the wisdom of the prophet Muhammad.

soft drugs a term sometimes used to describe drugs like cannabis or LSD that do not usually result in physical dependency. However, the term can be very misleading because people can still have problems using so-called 'soft drugs' (including psychological dependence).

stimulants (or 'uppers') these drugs make things seem as if they are happening faster, including what people are thinking, saying and doing.

strategic development plan a plan for long-term social and economic development.

street person usually a homeless person living on the street who has no proper address and is unemployed.

synthetic made by means of a chemical process.

trafficking the transportation and sale of something (i.e. illegal drugs) that should not be bought and sold.

transit country a country through which illegal drugs are carried from a producer country to a consumer country.

United Nations Drug Control Programme (UNDCP) part of the United Nations Office for Drug Control and Crime Prevention; the major international forum through which countries worldwide co-operate on drug control issues.

BOOKS TO READ

Forbidden Drugs
Philip Robson
(Oxford University Press, 2001)

Oxfam Country Profile: Bolivia
(Oxfam, 2001)

Oxfam Country Profile: Afghanistan
(Oxfam, 1998)

Why do People Take Drugs?
Patsy Westcott
(Hodder Wayland, 2001)

Drugs: Face the Facts series
(Hodder Wayland, 1996)

It Happened to Me: Drug Addict
(Franklin Watts, 2002)

SOURCES

Cocaine: An unauthorised biography
Dominic Streatfeild
(Virgin Publishing, 2001)

**Conflict and Consensus: European responses
to the international drugs trade**
(Catholic Institute for International Relations,
1998)

**Drugs, Trafficking and Criminal Policy:
The Scapegoat Strategy**
Penny Green
(Waterside Press, 1998)

**Families in the War on Drugs:
Peasant families, alternative development
and the war on drugs in Bolivia**
Pien Metaal
(Catholic Institute for International
Relations, 2001)

WEBSITES

For additional topics that are relevant to this book go to
www.waylinks.co.uk/series/21debates/drugstrade

USEFUL ADDRESSES

In the UK

DrugScope
32-36 Loman Street
London SE1 0EE
Tel: 020 7928 1211

Alcohol Concern
32-36 Loman Street
London SE1 0EE
Tel: 020 7928 7377

Health Education Board for Scotland
Woodburn House
Canaan Lane
Edinburgh EH10 4SG
Tel: 0131 536 5500

Catholic Institute for International Development
Unit 3, Canonbury Yard
190a North Road
London N1 7BJ

In the USA

Drug Enforcement Administration
Information Services Section (CPI)2401
Jefferson Davis Highway
Alexandria, VA 22301

National Institute on Drug Abuse
National Institute of Health
6001 Executive Boulevard,
Room 5213
Bethesda,
MD 20892-9561

In Australia

Alcohol and Other Drugs Council of Australia
PO Box 269, WODEN, ACT, 2606
17 Napier Close, Deakin, ACT, 2605
Tel: (02) 6281 0686

In Denmark

Danish Drug Users Union
Korsgade 30 3, 2200
Copenhagen N
Denmark

INDEX

Numbers in **bold** refer to illustrations.

addiction 6, 8, 9, 14, 15, 16, 18, 36, 37, 41, 42, **55**, 56, 58, 59
  genetic inclination to 38, 40
  psychological dependency 14, 15, 16, 19
Afghanistan 4, 20, 22, 23, **23**, 24, 27, 29, 32, 33, **33**, 38, **38**, 49
Africa 34, 35
alcohol 6, 8, 17, 36, 38, 40
amphetamines ('uppers') 5, 14, 16, 27, 43
amphetamine-type stimulants (ATS) 14, 34, 37, 59
appetite 15, 16
Arango, Luis Fernando 46
Arellano Felix, Ramon and Benjamin 30, **30**
Australia and New Zealand 37, 43

Balkans 29, 32
blood pressure 14, 15
Bolivia 4, 7, 20, 24, 25, 45, **50**, 51
  Dignity Plan 26, 50
Brazil 54
Bush, George (Snr) 44

caffeine 6
cannabis 5, 7, **7**, 8, 10, 14, 15, **15**, **26**, 27, 28, 30, 33, 36, 37, **37**, 38, 43, 48, 53, 58, **58**
Caribbean, the 7, 9, 29, 31
cartels, drug 30
cash crops 20, 48
Catholic Institue for International Relations (CIIR) 50
China 9, 29, 43
cigarettes *see* tobacco
coca 4, 7, 15, 20, 22, 24, 25, **25**, 26, 27, 38, **44**, 46, **46**, 48, 50, **50**, 51
Coca-Cola 8
cocaine 5, **5**, 7, 8, 10, 11, 12, 13, 15, 16, 20, 24, 25, **25**, 28, **28**, 29, 30, 31, 33, 34, **35**, 36, 37, 38, 40, 41, 43, **44**, 56
cocoa **49**
Colombia 7, 20, 22, 24, 25, **25**, 27, **28**, 29, 30, 33, **44**, 45, **46**, **47**, 51, 54, **54**
couriers 29, 31, 34
crack 7, 15, 43, 54, 58
crime 11, **11**, 29, 30, 34, 35, 36, 37, 40, 56, 57, **57**
customs officers 31, **31**, **35**, 43

DEA (Drug Enforcement Agency [US]) 11, 12, 58
decriminalization 56, 58
Denmark 43
depression 14, 16, **42**
drug barons 29, 30, **30**

ecstasy 14, 16, **17**, 27, **31**, 43
education **12**, 52, 53, **53**, 59
ergot fungus 19

FARC (Revolutionary Armed Forces of Colombia) 22, 45, **45**
farmers **4**, 20, 21, **21**, 22, **25**, 26, 27, 29, 46, 47, **47**, 48, **49**, 50, **50**
France **31**
fumigation 46, **46**

globalization 29
glue sniffing 9
'Golden Crescent' 22
'Golden Triangle' 24, 43
guerrilla movements 22, 24, 45

Haiti **35**
hallucinogens 15, 19
hashish 15
health problems 6, 12, 14, 15, 16, 18, 19, 37
heart disease 6, 16
hepatitis C 12, 16, 18, 42
heroin 5, 8, 10, 11, 12, 13, 18, **18**, 20, 22, 23, 24, 27, 28, 32, 33, 34, 36, 37, 38, 40, **40**, 41, 42, 43, **47**, 53, 54, **55**, 56, 58, 59
history of drug use 8, 9
HIV 12, 16, 18, 38, **40**, 55
homelessness **10**, 36, **36**, 54, 56
Houston (USA) **11**

injecting drugs 10, 14, 16, 17, 18, **18**, 38, 40, **40**, 55
Iran 22, 29, 32, **32**, 33, **33**
Italy 30

Jamaica 27, 31, 33
Japan 14

Korea, Republic of 14

Laos 24
legalization of drugs 13, 56, 57, 58
liver failure 6
London 5, 24, **36**, **40**, 43, **57**
  Lambeth 58, 59
LSD 19, **19**, 28, 58
lung cancer 6

Mafia 30
Manchester (UK) **26**
marijuana *see* cannabis
mental illness 16, 17, 19
metamphetamine 14
Mexico 27, 29, 30, **30**, 33
money laundering 35
Morocco 27, 30, 33
morphine 18
'mules' 31, 32
multiple sclerosis 38
Muslims 8
Myanmar 22, 24, 29, 38, **39**, 43, 49
  Wa rebels 22, 24

Netherlands 27, 55, 58, **58**
New York 5, **10**, 11, 24, 43
Nigeria 34, **34**, 35

Observer newspaper (UK) 46
opiates 15, 18, 29, 31, 32, 37, 59
opium 8, 9, **9**, 18, 20, 22, 23, **23**, 24, 25, 27, 29, 32, 33, 38, **38**, **39**, 43, **47**, 48
overdose 18

Pakistan 22, 23, 27, 29, **55**
Peru **4**, 7, 20, **21**, 24, 25, 45, **49**
Philippines 14
Poland 27
poppies *see* opium
Portugal 58, 59
poverty 44, 54, 56
prescription drugs 6, 17, 36
prohibition 13
Prozac 6
psychotherapy 56

respiratory problems 15, 16
Russia 30

Saudi Arabia 8
schizophrenia 19
sleeplessness 14
smoking *see* tobacco
South Africa 7
Spain 30, 33

Taiwan 14
Taliban 23, **23**, 38
teenagers 39, 40, **42**, 52, 53, **59**
Thailand 14, 24, 27, **34**, 49
tobacco 6, **6**, 15, 38, 40
tranquillizers 17
treatment programmes, drug addiction 55, 56
Turkey 29, 32, 49

UK 5, 6, 11, 20, 24, **26**, 28, **31**, 36, **36**, 39, 40, **40**, 43, 54, 55, 56, **57**, 58
United Nations (UN) 11, 29, 35, 47, 49, 56
  definition of illegal drugs 6
United Nations Drug Control Programme (UNDCP) 5, 36, 47
United Nations Office for Drug Control and Crime Prevention (UNODCCP) 27
USA 5, 6, 10, **10**, 11, **11**, 12, 13, 15, 20, 24, 25, 27, **28**, 29, 30, 33, 34, **35**, 37, 43, 44, **44**, 45, **47**, 54, 55, 56, 58

Valium 6
Vietnam 43

Wa rebels (Myanmar) 22, 24
'war on drugs' 4, 10, 11, 44, **46**, **47**
Whitear, Rachel 52
withdrawal symptoms 18